S⚽ccer Inspired
Physics & Engineering
Activities for Kids

Discover the Hidden Physics and Engineering Behind Your Favorite Sport

BOB MATHER

DISCLAIMER

Table of Contents

Introduction 5

Conservation of Momentum in Soccer 7

The Beauty of a Ground Pass 19

Flight of the Soccer Balls: The Projectile Trajectory 30

How The Soccer Wind Can Blow Your Mind 40

How a Soccer Ball Bends Through the Air 47

How the Goalkeeper Shuts You Down –
The Goalkeeping Glove Impact 55

Angled Shots: The More You See, the More you Score 62

Bonus: What a Drag 82

Conclusion 85

Challenge Answers 88

Introduction

Soccer, or football as it is recognised in many parts of the world, is the most popular sport on the planet. Millions of fans around the globe watch great players and teams compete at the highest level, with the FIFA World Cup being one of the most broadly watched events in the world. Beyond the excitement of the game, there are endless lessons to be learnt from soccer that can be utilized to different areas of life, including engineering.

Engineering is a vast and complex field that encompasses a wide variety of disciplines, from mechanical and electrical engineering to materials science. At its core, engineering is about problem solving that make our lives better. Whether it's designing a new product, building a bridge, or creating a software program application, engineering requires creativity, critical thinking, and a deep appreciation for the standards and techniques that underpin the field. Both soccer and engineering require a great deal of teamwork, adaptability and goal setting, in addition to skill, motivation and dedication.

In this book, we'll focus on a few basic principles of engineering that apply to soccer. We investigate how engineering principles affect the behavior of the soccer ball, soccer gloves and the techniques of soccer players. This book is great for soccer fans to learn more about their favorite sport, and also for those who want to better understand some of the basic principles in engineering.

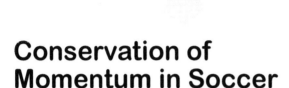

Conservation of Momentum in Soccer

If you watch or play soccer, you might wonder why a ball moves the way it does. Why does the ball move faster in some instances and go farther? Why does it bounce higher sometimes? In this chapter, we'll take a closer look at the behavior of the soccer ball after it is kicked. We'll use physics to determine the velocity of the ball when it is kicked. And also have a look at other factors that can affect the trajectory of the ball.

First, let's look at momentum.

The momentum of an object is its mass times velocity.

$$p = mv$$

Where p is the momentum, m is the mass and v is the velocity.

When a player kicks a soccer ball, he transfers momentum onto the soccer ball. Like everything in nature, soccer also follows the laws of physics, and in this case, the law of conservation of momentum.

According to the law of conservation of momentum, in a closed system, when two objects collide, the total momentum remains the same.

So, when a player kicks a ball, the total momentum of the player and ball before the kick is equal to the total momentum of the player and ball after the kick.

$$P_{i,ball} + P_{i,player} = P_{f,ball} + P_{f,player}$$

$p_{i,ball}$ = Initial momentum of ball

$p_{i,player}$ = Initial momentum of player

$p_{f,ball}$ = Final momentum of ball

$p_{f,player}$ = Final momentum of player

Before Kick

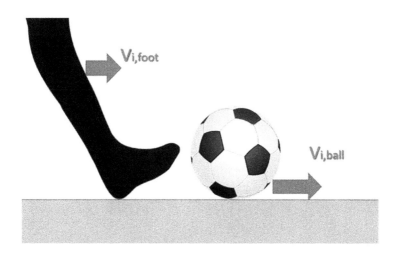

After Kick

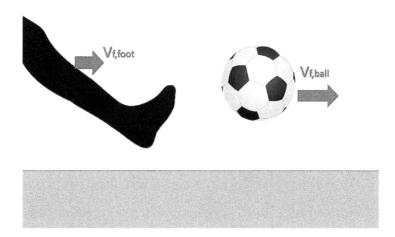

Using the first momentum equation and plugging into the 2nd equation, we get:

$$m_{ball} * v_{i,ball} + m_{player} * v_{i,player}$$

$$= m_{ball} * v_{f,ball} + m_{player} * v_{f,player}$$

m_{ball} = Mass of ball

m_{player} = Mass of player

$v_{i,ball}$ = Initial velocity of ball

$v_{i,player}$ = Initial velocity of player

$v_{f,ball}$ = Final velocity of ball

$v_{f,player}$ = Final velocity of player

But let's keep in mind that the only part of the player's body kicking the ball is the foot. So, we care about the mass and velocity of the foot. We also use a term known as effective mass of the foot. This is the standalone mass of the portion of the foot that strikes the soccer ball. There are many forces generated by the muscles during the kick that gives it a higher mass than the other standing foot. So, the equation now becomes:

$$m_{ball} * v_{i,ball} + m_{foot,effective} * v_{i,foot}$$

$$= m_{ball} * v_{f,ball} + m_{foot,effective} * v_{f,foot}$$

m_{ball} = Mass of ball

$m_{foot,effective}$ = Effective mass of foot

$v_{i,ball}$ = Initial velocity of ball

$v_{i,foot}$ = Initial velocity of foot

$v_{f,ball}$ = Final velocity of ball

$v_{f,foot}$ = Final velocity of foot

Now, let's look at a simple example.

The mass of a soccer ball is 410 grams (0.41 kg). It is at rest, so it has an initial velocity of zero.

Let's assume that a soccer player kicks a ball. Let's assume his foot has an effective mass of 1 kg and his foot is moving at a velocity of 20 m/s.

The velocity of the foot after kicking the ball is 5 m/s. So, let's use this data in above formula to calculate velocity of the ball.

Before Kick

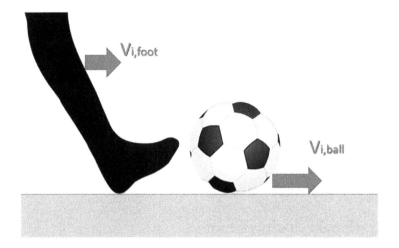

After Kick

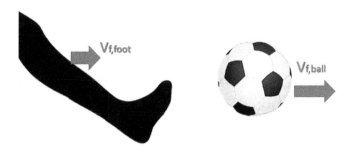

$$m_{ball} * v_{i,ball} + m_{foot,effective} * v_{i,foot}$$
$$= m_{ball} * v_{f,ball} + m_{foot,effective} * v_{f,foot}$$

$m_{ball} = 0.41 \text{ kg}$

$m_{foot,effective} = 1 \text{ kg}$

$v_{i,ball} = 0 \text{ m/s}$

$v_{i,foot} = 20 \text{ m/s}$

$v_{f,ball} = ??$

$v_{f,foot} = 5 \text{ m/s}$

$$0.41 * 0 + 1 * 20 = 0.41 * v_{f,ball} + 1 * 5$$

$$v_{f,ball} = 36.6 \text{ m/s}$$

As we can see, the final velocity of the ball is 36.6 m/s as some of the momentum from the foot is transferred to the ball.

Elasticity

Now, let's look at the conservation of momentum equation again… "According to the law of conservation of momentum, in a closed system, when two objects collide, the total momentum remains the same."

When we did the previous calculations, we assumed that the player and ball are in a "closed system". But is that true? A closed system means nothing else is interacting between the player and ball. But in real life, there is friction, heat loss, wind etc. that affects the momentum of the ball. Friction is two surfaces rubbing against each other.

What happens is that there is a slight loss in momentum due to above factors. So, the final momentum is slightly less than the initial momentum. This loss in momentum is indicated by a factor known as elasticity. In equation below, the initial momentum is multiplied by an elasticity factor e that is less than 1.

$$(p_{i,ball} + p_{i,player}) * e = (p_{f,ball} + p_{fi,player})$$

If e=1; it indicates a perfectly inelastic collision between player and ball. However, in real life e is less than 1.

$$(m_{ball} * v_{i,ball} + m_{foot,effective} * v_{i,foot}) * e = e * (m_{ball} * v_{f,ball} + m_{foot,effective} * v_{f,foot})$$

Let's look at same example above taking into account an elasticity e of 0.95.

Before Kick

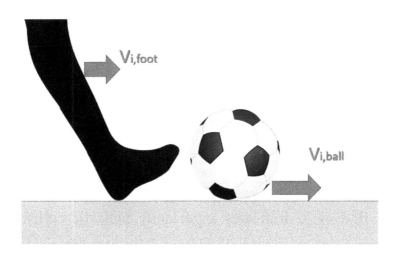

After Kick

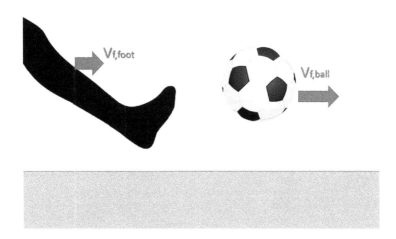

m_{ball} = 0.41 kg

$m_{foot,effective}$ = 1 kg

$v_{i,ball}$ = 0 m/s

$v_{i,foot}$ = 20 m/s

$v_{f,ball}$ = ??

$v_{f,foot}$ = 5 m/s

$$(0.41 * 0 + 1 * 20) * 0.95 = (0.41 * v_{f,ball} + 1 * 5)$$

$$v_{f,ball} = 34.14 \ m/s$$

The final velocity of the ball is **34.14 m/s** which is lower than the first calculation of 36.6 m/s. This is because some of the energy is lost to the environment due to heat, friction etc. This is because the player-ball system is not a completely open system, and we need to take elasticity into account.

Now, here's an example of you to practice:

Challenge 1:

The mass of a soccer ball is 410 grams (0.41 kg). It is moving slowly, with an initial velocity of 2 m/s in the same direction of the kick.

The soccer player kicks a ball. His foot has an effective mass of 1 kg, and his foot is moving at a velocity of 10 m/s.

The velocity of the foot after kicking is 7 m/s. The elasticity of the system is 0.92. Calculate the final velocity of the ball.

The Beauty of a
Ground Pass

A ground pass is among the most fundamental skills in soccer. A team that plays a ground passing game is the best to watch. An Arsenal, Barcelona or Manchester City seems more attractive to watch than a Liverpool. The beauty lies in the effectiveness, simplicity and creativity used to unlock the tightest of defences and create goal scoring opportunities. It requires a precise weighting of the pass, close control and fast runs from teammates.

In this section, we'll have a look at how fast a ball moves for a ground pass. We'll look at the forces acting on the ball and how it affects the speed and acceleration of the soccer ball.

Before we get started, let's define Newton's second law of motion, which states that "the acceleration of an object is dependent on two variables, the external force acting on the object and the mass of the object."

In the case of a ground pass, there is a kicking force acting in the horizontal direction (we'll call this the x-axis). And there is no external force acting on the ball in the vertical direction (the y-axis).

To describe all the forces acting on the ball, we use something known as the free body diagram. A free body diagram is a simplified version of all forces acting on an object at a particular moment in time.

The Free body diagram of the soccer ball is below.

In the vertical direction, the weight of the soccer ball W acts downwards, and there is a reaction force F_n that the ground exerts on the ball in the upward direction.

The player exerts a kicking force F_k on the ball to the right in the horizontal direction. This induces a frictional force f_s between the ground and the ball in the opposite direction. Friction is the force generated by two surfaces rubbing against each other.

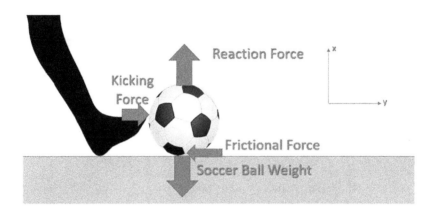

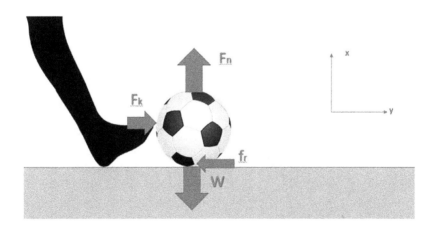

In the free body diagram, we sum all the forces in the two directions to solve the problem.

x-direction:

In the x-direction, we have two forces acting, the kicking force F_k and the frictional force f_s. The resultant force creates motion to the right. Let the acceleration of the ball to the right be a_x. Now, based on Newton's second law of motion, we get:

$$F_k - f_s = m\, a_x$$

Where **m** is the mass of the ball

y-direction:

In the y-direction, we have two forces acting, the weight of the ball W and the reaction force F_n. The resultant force doesn't create any motion up or down, so acceleration in the y-direction is 0. Now, based on Newton's second law of motion, we get:

$$F_n - W = 0$$

$$F_n = W$$

The reaction force is equal and opposite to the weight of the ball.

Now that we know all the forces acting on the ball, let's have a look at each of them individually:

Weight of Ball W

The weight of the ball is the force exerted due to gravity on the ball. So, the force exerted downwards on the ball is the mass of the ball m times the acceleration due to gravity g.

$W = m * g$

The value of g was determined to be 9.81 m/s^2 on earth by great philosopher Isaac Newton.

Normal Reaction Force F_n

Now, if there was no force acting upwards on the ball, it would just rip through the earth and fly off into the solar system on the other side. However, there is a force acting upwards that is just enough to keep it stable vertically. The force is not too high to prevent it from moving upwards. This force is known as the normal reaction force F_n.

Frictional Force f_s

When a ball is kicked horizontally on the ground, we know that it eventually comes to rest no matter how hard it is kicked. This is because there is a force acting on the ball in a direction opposite to motion. This force is caused by the interaction between the ball and the grass and is called frictional force. The rougher the surface, the higher the frictional force and the faster the ball stops. That's why you see that the soccer ball stops faster on a sandy surface versus a smooth glass surface.

That's because the sandy surface has a higher coefficient of friction μ. The coefficient of friction μ is a property of the surface. A polished smooth glass surface has a coefficient of friction of almost zero, so you see that the ball barely slows down on the glass surface when it is rolled on a glass surface. The formula for frictional force is below:

$$f_s = \mu F_n$$

The frictional force depends on the coefficient of friction of the surface and the normal reaction of the surface. When we plug in the value of the normal reaction force below, we get the value of f_s:

$$f_s = \mu W = \mu mg$$

So, the heavier the ball and the rougher the surface, the higher the frictional force and the faster the ball stops.

Now, let's apply the information to the forces in y-direction:

$$F_n = W$$

$$F_n = m^*g$$

And, in the x-direction we get:

$$F_k - f_s = m\,a_x$$

$$F_k - \mu\,mg = m\,a_x$$

$$\mathbf{F_k = \mu\,mg + m\,a_x}$$

Or

$$\mathbf{a_x = F_k/m - \mu\,g}$$

So, we see that a larger force creates a larger acceleration along the ground. A higher coefficient of friction and a heavier ball both reduce acceleration.

Now, let's look at a simple example.

Ronaldo kicks a stationary ball along the ground with a force of 150 N. The ball weighs 0.41 kg and they are playing on a soccer field with a coefficient of friction of 0.62 between the grass and the ball. What's the acceleration of the ball?

F_k = Force on the ball = 150 N

m = mass of the ball = 0.41 kg

μ = Coefficient of static friction = 0.62

g = acceleration due to gravity = 9.81 m/s²

Now, using the acceleration equation, we get:

$a_x = F_k/m - \mu g$

$=150/0.41 - 0.61*9.8$

=359.9 m/s²

Now, that we have the acceleration of the kick, what is the velocity of the ball after 2 seconds on the ground?

We know that the acceleration is the change in velocity over time.

$a_x = (v_x - u_x)/t$

where:

v_x = Final velocity after 2 seconds = ??

u_x = Initial velocity of stationary ball = 0

t = time = 2 seconds

Now, let's plug these values into the formula

$a_x = (v_x - u_x)/t$

$359.9 = (v_x - 0)/2$

$v_x = 719.8$ m/s

The velocity after 2 seconds is **719.8** m/s.

And here's the free body diagram for the kick…

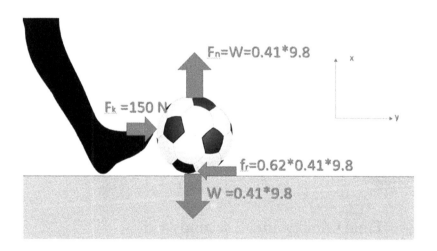

Exercises

Challenge 2

Now, it's your turn.

Messi passes a stationary ball along the ground with a force of 100 N. The ball weighs 0.41 kg and they are playing on a soccer field with a coefficient of friction of 0.7 between the grass and the ball. What's the acceleration of the ball? Fill in the free body diagram below while solving the problem.

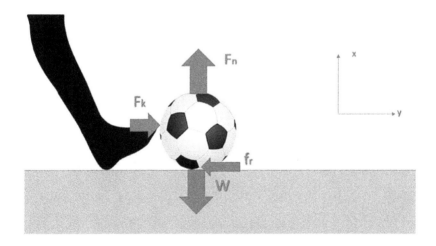

Flight of the Soccer Balls: The Projectile Trajectory

The flight of a soccer ball is an incredibly beautiful sight. The skills of the midfielder who can kick a ball at just the right angle of elevation and pace to catch the run of the offensive player is a marvel to watch. David Beckham was a master of the long pass. There's even a goal he's made from the halfway line.

When a soccer ball is kicked in the air, it follows the path of a projectile. The larger the angle of elevation of the kick, and the faster the velocity of the kick, the higher and farther it goes.

It is possible to calculate the maximum height and range from the initial velocity and angle of the kick. And we can also calculate the time the soccer ball is in the air.

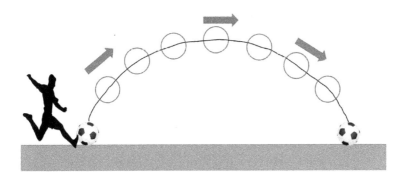

Let's say that the soccer ball is kicked at a speed of u m/s at an angle of elevation of Θ. It follows the projectile trajectory below with a maximum height H and a range of R.

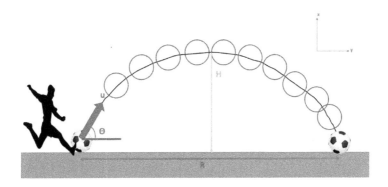

The velocity u can be broken down into horizonal and vertical components using trigonometry. Breaking this down helps us to get a horizontal and vertical component. Let's say that the horizontal component of velocity u is u_x and the vertical component is u_y

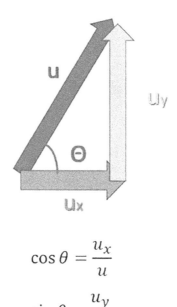

$$\cos \theta = \frac{u_x}{u}$$

$$\sin \theta = \frac{u_y}{u}$$

Now, we get values for u_x and u_y below by cross multiplying:

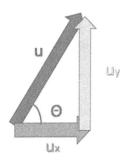

$$u_x = u \cos \theta$$
$$u_y = u \sin \theta$$

Now, after inserting these values into the diagram, we get the updated diagram below:

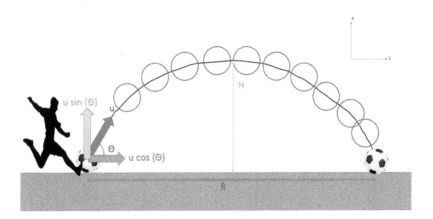

So, once we apply our force calculation in the x-direction and y-direction, we get the below values for horizontal range R and maximum height H. The details of how we get these 3 equations are beyond the scope of this book.

$$H = \frac{u^2 (sin\ \theta)^2}{2g}$$

$$R = \frac{u^2 \sin 2\theta}{g}$$

$$t = \frac{2u \sin \theta}{g}$$

Now, let's look at an example:

Fred kicks the soccer ball at 20 m/s at an angle of elevation of 30 degrees. How long is the ball in the air, and how long does it travel? What's the maximum height achieved?

To solve this, first let's draw the diagram of the ball with the relevant data.

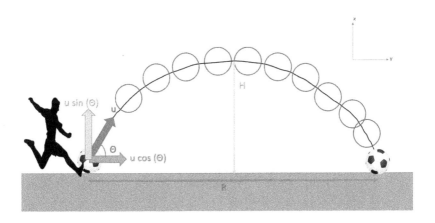

We know from the data that:

u=20 m/s

Θ = 30 degrees

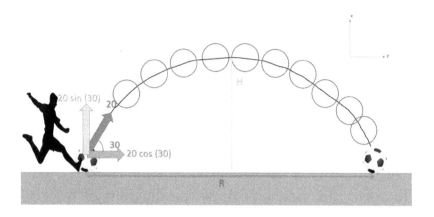

Based on the equation for maximum vertical height, we get:

$$H = \frac{u^2 \, (sin \, \theta)^2}{2g}$$

$$H = \frac{20^2 \, (sin \, 30)^2}{2 * 9.8} = 5.1 \; m \; high$$

Based on the equation for horizontal range, we get:

$$R = \frac{u^2 \, sin \, 2\theta}{g}$$

$$R = \frac{20^2 \, sin \, 60}{9.8} = 35.35 \; m$$

Based on the equation for time of flight we get:

$$t = \frac{2u \sin \theta}{g}$$

$$H = \frac{2 * 20 \sin 30}{9.8} = 2.04 \; seconds$$

So, the ball travels in the air 35.35 m long in 2.04 seconds. It achieves a maximum height of 5.1 m before coming down.

Now, it's time for a practice exercise for you...

Challenge 3

Tim kicks a soccer ball with an initial speed of 10 m/s at an angle of elevation of 45 degrees. Fill out the diagram below and figure out how far the ball goes, and the maximum height it can achieve.

Bonus: Is it going to fly over a goalpost 10 m away? (Hint: The height of a goalpost is 2.7 m)

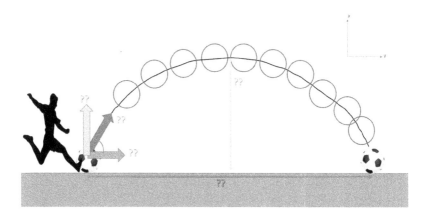

A Short message from the Author

Hey, are you enjoying the book? I'd love to hear your thoughts!

Many readers do not know how hard reviews are to come by, and how much they help an author.

I would be incredibly thankful if you could take just 60 seconds to write a brief review on Amazon, even if it's just a few sentences!

Browse to the product page and leave a review as shown below.

Thank you for taking the time to share your thoughts!

Your review will genuinely make a difference for me and help gain exposure for my work.

How The Soccer Wind Can Blow Your Mind

In the previous chapter, "Flight of the Soccer Ball" we calculated the projectile motion of a soccer ball kicked with a certain velocity. However, there's one thing missing. The wind.

The wind complicates things a little. If the wind blows in the direction of the soccer ball, it increases the speed of the ball. If the wind blows in the opposite direction of the ball, it decreases the speed of the ball.

There are two terms that we need to understand to move forward, relative velocity and absolute velocity.

Absolute velocity is the velocity of the ball assuming that the wind speed is zero. In the previous chapter, we used only absolute velocity as we didn't consider the wind speed.

Relative velocity is the velocity of the ball considering the velocity of the wind. The wind speed slows down or speeds up the relative velocity of the ball depending on the actual direction of the wind.

Ball moving in direction of wind.

As mentioned, when the ball moves in direction of wind, there is an increase in speed due to the wind.

The relative velocity of the ball is just the velocity of the ball plus the velocity of the wind. This increase in velocity means that the ball travels further horizontally than it otherwise would.

As seen in the diagram below, the relative velocity of the ball ($V_{ball,rel}$) is velocity of the ball (V_{ball}) plus velocity of the wind(V_{wind}).

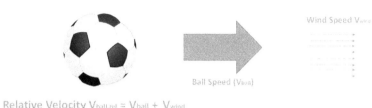

Relative Velocity $V_{ball,rel} = V_{ball} + V_{wind}$
Absolute Velocity $V_{ball,abs} = V_{ball}$

Ball Moving Against the Wind

When the ball is going against the wind, the ball slows down. The relative velocity of the ball decreases by the velocity of the wind. The relative velocity of the wind is just the velocity of the ball V_{ball} minus the velocity of the wind V_{wind}.

Relative Velocity $V_{ball,rel} = V_{ball} - V_{wind}$
Absolute Velocity $V_{ball,abs} = V_{ball}$

This might seem like a simple concept to some, but it's very important to get the simple concepts right before moving on to advanced concepts.

Now, let's look at a few simple examples.

Ball in Direction of Wind - Example

A ball is moving at a velocity of 27 mph in the direction of wind. The wind is blowing at 10 mph. What is the absolute velocity and relative velocity of the ball?

$$V_{ball} = 27 \text{ mph}$$

$$V_{wind} = 10 \text{ mph}$$

$$V_{ball,rel} = ??$$

$$V_{ball,abs} = ??$$

V_{wind} = Wind Speed = 10 mph

V_{ball} = Ball Speed = 27 mph

$V_{ball,rel}$ = 27+10 = 37 mph

$V_{ball,abs}$ = 27 mph

Ball in Opposite Direction of Wind - Example

A ball is moving at a velocity of 27 mph in the direction of wind. The wind is blowing in the opposite direction at 10 mph. What is the absolute velocity and relative velocity of the ball?

V_{ball} = 27 mph

V_{wind} = 10 mph

$V_{ball,rel}$ = ??

$V_{ball,abs}$ = ??

V_{wind} = Wind Speed = 10 mph

V_{ball} =Ball Speed = 27 mph

$V_{ball,rel}$ = 27-10 = 17 mph
$V_{ball,abs}$ = 27 mph

Practical Exercises

Now, it's time for a few practical exercises for you. For each of the below exercises, solve the problem by filling in the diagrams below:

Challenge 4:

The ball is moving at a speed of 20 mph. The wind is blowing against the ball at a speed of 10 mph. What's the absolute and relative velocity of the ball?

$V_{ball} = $ Ball Speed = ??

$V_{ball,rel} = $??
$V_{ball,abs} = $??

Challenge 5:

A ball is moving at a velocity of 37 mph in the direction of wind. The wind is blowing at 10 mph. What is the absolute velocity and relative velocity of the ball?

$V_{ball} = $ Ball Speed = ??

$V_{ball,rel} = $??
$V_{ball,abs} = $??

How a Soccer Ball Bends Through the Air

There's no more beautiful sight in soccer than to see a soccer ball curve in the air towards the top corner of the goal. The goalkeeper thinks the ball is going out due to the trajectory observed. However, it starts curving in midway through the shot and eventually reaches the top corner.

The goalkeeper and defence lie stunned, marvelling at what just happened, while the striker celebrates with his teammates. The skill and precision of the striker is celebrated across the world as a soccer genius. The hours of practice have started to pay off.

The beauty of the moment is due to the interaction between the ball and the atmosphere. The arc of the ball seems to follow the motion of a graceful dance, as it weaves its way across goalkeepers and defenders and finds its way to the top corner. It seems to defy the laws of physics and the laws of gravity.

The Soccer Ball follows a principle known as Bernoulli's theorem, which states that pressure in a fluid (such as air) is inversely proportional to the velocity of the fluid. So, a higher pressure at one point of the fluid means that it has a lower velocity at that point. The difference in pressure causes the ball to move towards the lower pressure surface. It's the same principle on which aeroplanes fly.

In soccer, when a ball is kicked in the air, there is a velocity differential between one side and the other. The side that is moving into the direction of the wind has a lower velocity than the opposite side. This is because the wind must curve more to reach the opposite side. The air facing the wind just glides across the surface at a lower velocity.

According to Bernoulli's theorem, a side with lower velocity has higher pressure and a side with higher velocity has lower pressure. The pressure difference causes a bending force from a direction of higher pressure towards the direction of lower pressure. This force is also called a magnus force and causes the ball to bend. This phenomenon is explained in the diagram below.

See diagrams below.

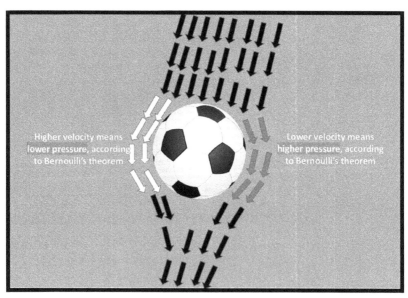

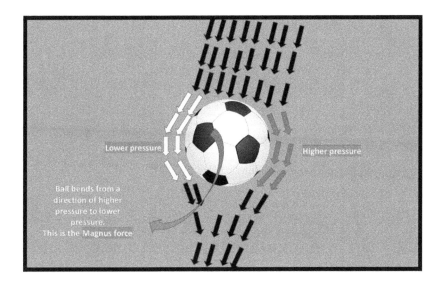

Other factors to consider:

1. **Location of ball contact with foot:** When the ball is just leaving the ground, the area where the ball hits the foot has a higher pressure than the other side. This causes the ball to bend towards the opposite side initially. This is also the dominant factor when there is not much wind around.

2. **Speed of ball:** The faster the ball is moving through the air, the more the Magnus force, and the more it is likely to bend.

3. **Wind speed:** The faster the wind is pushing against the ball, the larger the Magnus force, and the more it is likely to bend.

Exercises:

Challenge 6:

Here's a few fun exercises for you to practice. Here's the ball with the wind flowing against it. In the empty sheet below, draw the areas of high and low pressure and the direction it is likely to bend.

The black areas represent the direction of the wind, and the white arrow is the direction the ball is moving.

Draw your answer in the sheet below:

Challenge 7:

Draw your answer below:

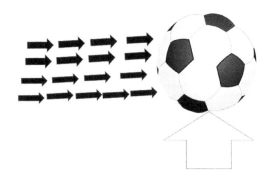

How the Goalkeeper Shuts You Down – The Goalkeeping Glove Impact

The goalkeeper is the reason why you can never seem to score. He's always there, blocking your shot, clearing the ball, punching it, and holding on to it. The goalkeeper is aware of everything that's happening on the soccer field, including movements of the opposing players, and making quick decisions on how to handle opposing players. He can communicate effectively with other players and maintain mental focus all throughout the game.

In this chapter, we're going to have a look at goalkeeping glove design. We see that the top of the glove above the fingers has extra padding. This extra padding makes it easier to punch the ball away. The padding absorbs the impact of the ball moving towards the fingers and offers extra protection to the fingers. Why does this happen? Let's investigate.

As we see below, the ball moves towards the gloves with a velocity and applies a force on the gloves.

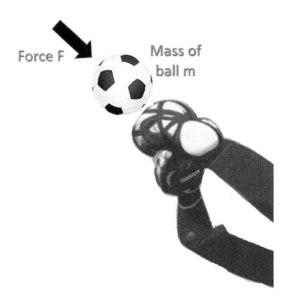

From the force equation, we know:

$$F = ma$$

$$F = \frac{m(v - u)}{t}$$

Where F is the force applied on the gloves

m is the mass of the ball

t is the time of contact between ball and gloves

v is final velocity

u is the initial velocity

In the above equation, the soft padding in the gloves increases the time of contact between ball and gloves. This extra time reduces the force that the ball applies on the gloves, and the force that the fingers feel. This increases the protection that the keeper's fingers get.

Now, let's look at an example.

Goalkeeper A decides he has superhuman hands and decides not to wear any gloves. Goalkeeper B is wearing regular goalkeeping gloves with padding. A ball of mass 0.41 kg hits both hands at 20 m/s and both keepers punch the ball back at 10 m/s (the ball is 10 m/s after the punch). The ball contacts Goalkeeper A's hands for 0.1 seconds while it is in contact with Goalkeeper B's gloves for 0.6 seconds. What is the force applied on Goalkeeper A's hands and Goalkeeper B's gloves?

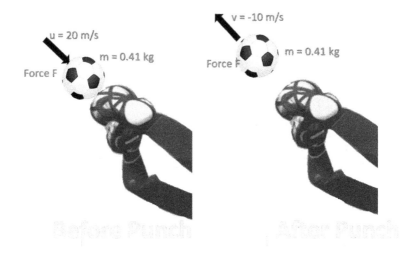

So, we have:

m = 0.41 kg

u = 20 m/s

v = -10 m/s (it goes in opposite direction so -ve sign)

$$F = \frac{m\,(v - u)}{t}$$

$$F_A = \frac{0.41\,(-10 - 20)}{0.1} = 123\ N$$

$$F_B = \frac{0.41(-10 - 20)}{0.6} = 20.5 \ N$$

The ball applies almost 1/6th the force on Goalkeeper B's gloves than it does on Goalkeeper A's hands. As we can see, there's a strong cushion effect for Goalkeeper B.

Challenge 8:

In the example above, the ball hits both hands at 50 m/s and both keepers punch the ball back at 10 m/s (the ball is 10 m/s after the punch). The ball contacts Goalkeeper A's hands for 0.05 seconds while it is in contact with Goalkeeper B's gloves for 0.5 seconds. What is the force applied on Goalkeeper A's hands and Goalkeeper B's gloves? Complete the free body diagram below and calculate.

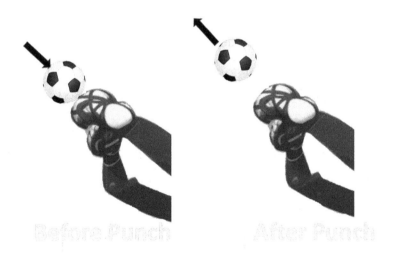

Angled Shots: The More You See, the More you Score

Young soccer players learn about the geometry of the game even before they enter the classroom. They learn that if they move the ball towards the center they get a better angle for the shot, and score more often.

Young defenders also learn that if they force the striker wide before shooting, they have a better chance of saving the goal.

Goalkeepers also learn to move forward to reduce the angle that the striker can see.

Let's have a look at an example below:

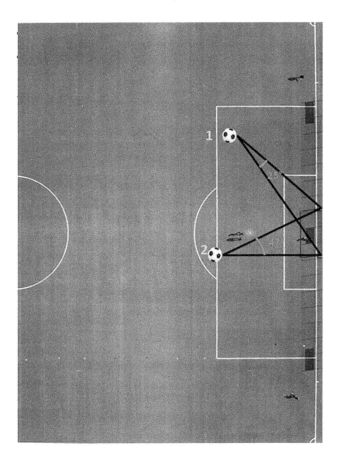

In diagram above, we look at two different positions marked 1 and 2. Position 1 has a 25 degrees angle view of the goal. position 2 has a 47 degree angle view of the goal.

Which position is better for scoring? Position 2 is much better than Position 1, assuming the player can shoot with both feet equally. The higher the angle, the better the position.

Sample Exercise:

Challenge 9:

Which of the below spots (1,2,3) are most likely to result in a goal?

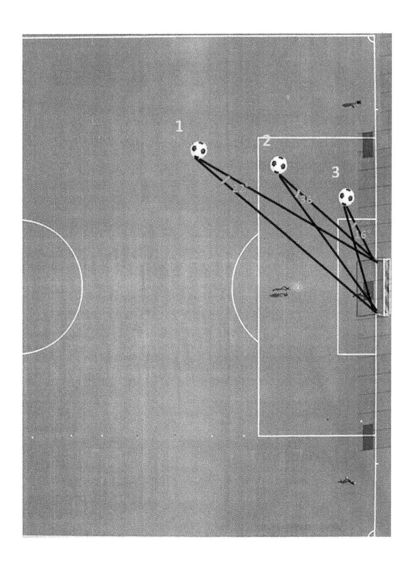

So, is there actually a way to calculate the angle? Yes, there is.

It uses Pythagros theorem below:

The Pythagros theorem states that in a right-angled triangle, the sum of the squares of the two sides of the right angle is equal to the square of the hypotenuse.

In the example below, *h* is the hypotenuse, *a* and *b* are the two sides of the right angle. Θ is the angle between the hypotenuse and side *b*

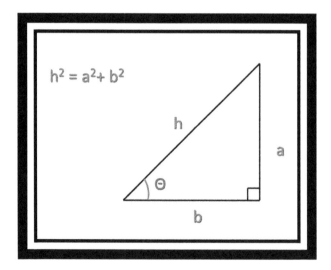

$$\sin \Theta = \frac{a}{h}$$

$$\cos \Theta = \frac{a}{h}$$

$$\tan \Theta = \frac{a}{h}$$

So, how does this work on the soccer field? Let's look at the diagram below.

The point where player contacts the ball forms two right angles with each post.

The orange triangle forms a right angle with the near post.

The blue triangle forms a right angle with the far post.

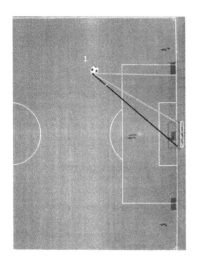 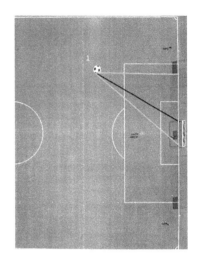

Now, let's say the spot is 25 m (75 ft) away horizontally and 15 m (45 m) away vertically from the near post.

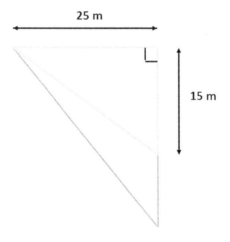

Now, if the goalpost is 7 m wide (or 21 feet wide), we get:

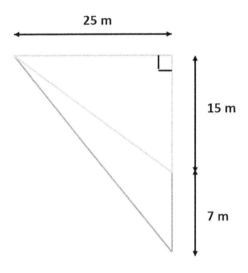

So, to solve this, we break it down into two triangles and find each angle.

First, let's do the orange triangle. In the orange triangle Θ^1 is the angle between the hypotenuse and the horizontal distance. We get Θ^1 as 30.96°.

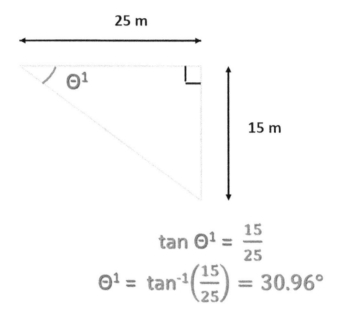

$$\tan \Theta^1 = \frac{15}{25}$$

$$\Theta^1 = \tan^{-1}\left(\frac{15}{25}\right) = 30.96°$$

Now, let's do the blue triangle. In the blue triangle Θ^2 is the angle between the hypotenuse and the horizontal distance. We get Θ^2 as 41.37°.

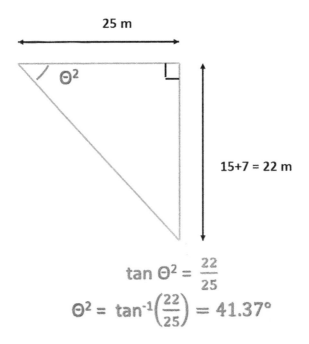

$$\tan \Theta^2 = \frac{22}{25}$$

$$\Theta^2 = \tan^{-1}\left(\frac{22}{25}\right) = 41.37°$$

Θ^1 and Θ^2 are shown in the diagram below.

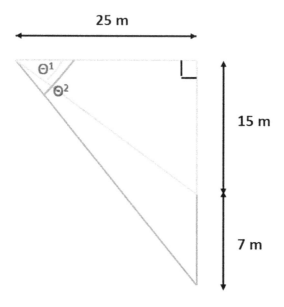

The difference between the two angles ($\Theta^2 - \Theta^1$) gives you the actual value of the angle between the posts.

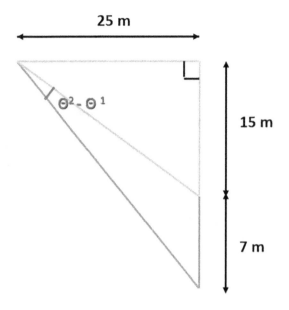

$\Theta^2 - \Theta^1$ is equal to $(41.37° - 30.96° = 11.41°)$

So, the angle between the two goal posts is **11.41°** for a point that's 25 m away horizontally and 15 m away vertically.

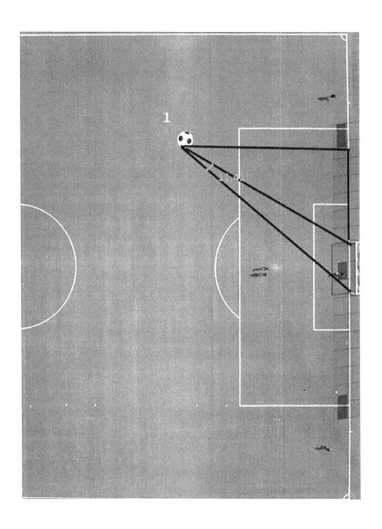

Challenge 10:

What is the angle that a spot makes between the goalposts? The spot is 15 m away horizontally and 15 m away vertically as shown below.

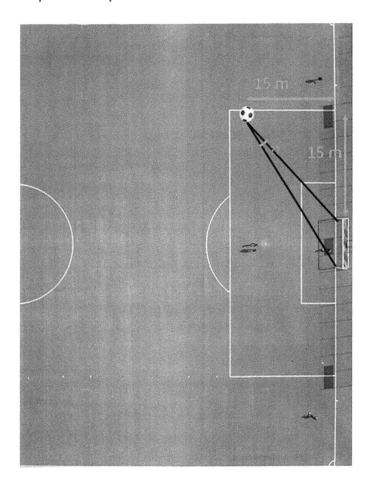

You can do your rough workings on sheet below…

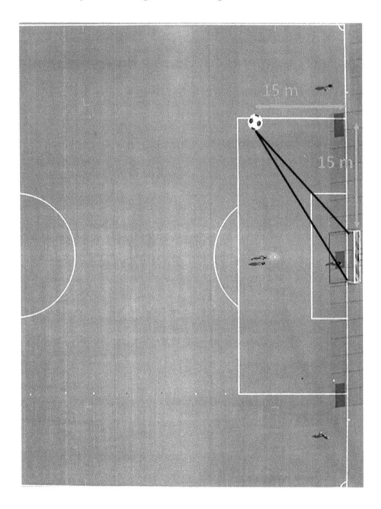

How the Keeper Fits Into This

You might have noticed plenty of times when the keeper has stepped out to get closer to the striker. This might strike you as a little strange. Doesn't the keeper have more time to see the ball and react if he stays backwards? Well, it's a bit more complicated than that.

You have just learnt how to calculate the shooting angle between the goal posts and the ball. However, one thing that calculation doesn't take into account is the goalkeeper. The goalkeeper is a small spot in the goal if he stays put. However, if the goalkeeper moves forward, he cuts into the angle a bit more; and the striker sees less of the ball.

The picture below explains this concept a bit more. The red lines are the portion of the goal that is blocked by the keeper. The area between the black and red lines is the area that the striker can score.

As we can see, when the keeper moves forward, the area available to score is much smaller, and this reduces the chances of a goal happening.

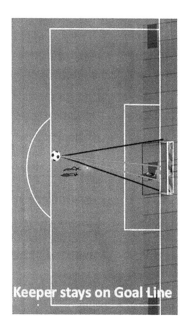
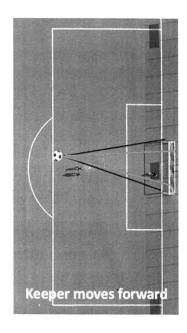

Also, the wider the keeper is able to stretch while moving forward, the more of the goal he can block. That's why we often see keepers stretch as wide as possible while facing a striker.

Practice Exercises

For the below diagrams, draw straight lines that show the viewing area of the goal; and the viewing area blocked by the goalkeeper.

Challenge 11:

Challenge 12:

Challenge 13:

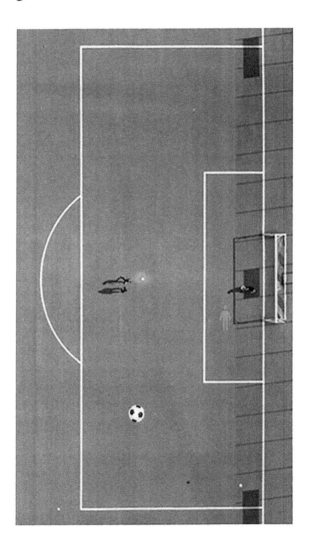

Bonus: What a Drag

What is Drag?

Drag is the air resistance experienced by the ball while it is moving through the air. It's like an extra force experienced by the ball in a direction opposite to the direction of motion.

This causes the ball to travel a shorter distance and move to a lower height.

Drag on a Soccer Ball

When a soccer ball moves through the air, the air separates along the surface of the soccer ball and moves over the back of the ball as shown below.

Behind the soccer ball, there is an area of turbulence called the wake of the flow. The wake of the soccer ball causes the drag force.

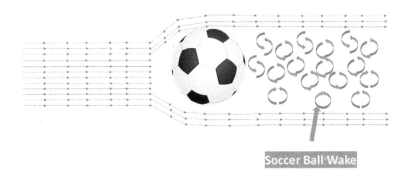

Soccer Ball Wake

Reduce Drag on Soccer Ball

One way to reduce drag on a soccer ball is to reduce the size of the wake behind the soccer ball. One strategy is to add more panels to the soccer ball, and this causes the wind to stick closer to the surface of the ball as it moves over. It reduces the size of the wake behind as shown below. Another way to increase this is to add dimples or find other ways to increase surface roughness.

This is also the reason that a golf ball has dimples on the surface.

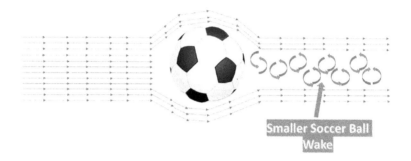

Smaller Soccer Ball Wake

Conclusion

Thank you for taking the time to read this book.

I hope you have found it useful; and learnt a few basic engineering concepts. If you've been through the exercises, you now understand the basics.

If you liked my book and you'd like to learn more, check out my Author page below. I have half a dozen books out on coding for kids and beginners.

https://www.amazon.com/Bob-Mather/e/ B07HHQZC4Y

If you like more books similar to this one, feel free to try these ones out below:

Fascinating Engineering Book for Kids: 500 Dynamic Facts

Awesome Engineering Activities for Kids

If you'd like any clarification regarding the topics; or any suggestions; please email me at: abiprod.pty.ltd@ gmail.com

I also do one-one coaching online if you are interested in personalized help.

The end... almost!

Reviews are not easy to come by.

As an independent author with a tiny marketing budget, I rely on readers, like you, to leave a short review on Amazon.

Even if it's just a sentence or two!

So if you enjoyed the book, please browse to the product page and leave a review as shown below:

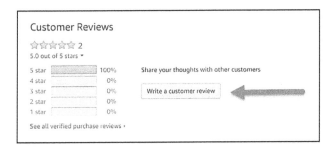

I am very appreciative for your review as it truly makes a difference.

Thank you from the bottom of my heart for purchasing this book and reading it to the end.

Challenge Answers

Challenge 1:

The mass of a soccer ball is 410 grams (0.41 kg). It is moving slowly, with an initial velocity of 2 m/s in the same direction of the kick.

The soccer player kicks a ball. His foot has an effective mass of 1 kg and his foot is moving at a velocity of 10 m/s.

The velocity of the foot after kicking is 7 m/s. The elasticity of the system is 0.92. Calculate the final velocity of the ball.

Challenge 1 Answer:

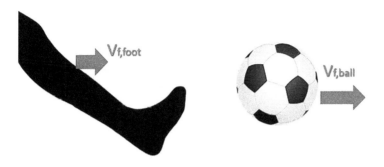

$m_{ball} = 0.41$ kg

$m_{foot,effective} = 1$ kg

$v_{i,ball} = 2$ m/s

$v_{i,foot} = 10$ m/s

$v_{f,ball} = ??$

$v_{f,foot} = 7$ m/s

$$(0.41 * 2 + 1 * 10) * 0.92 = (0.41 * v_{f,ball} + 1 * 7)$$
$$v_{f,ball} = 7.21 \ m/s$$

Challenge 2

Now, it's your turn.

Messi passes a stationary ball along the ground with a force of 100 N. The ball weighs 0.41 kg and they are playing on a soccer field with a coefficient of friction of 0.7 between the grass and the ball. What's the acceleration of the ball? Fill in the free body diagram below while solving the problem.

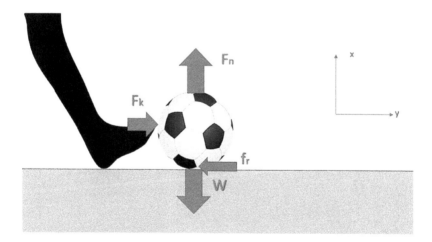

Challenge 2 – Answers

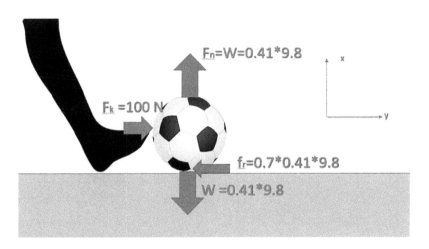

F_k = Force on the ball = 100 N

m = mass of the ball = 0.41 kg

μ = Coefficient of static friction = 0.7

g = acceleration due to gravity = 9.81 m/s²

$a_x = F_k/m - \mu g$

=100/0.41 – 0.7*9.8

=237 m/s²

Challenge 3

Tim kicks a soccer ball with an initial speed of 10 m/s at an angle of elevation of 45 degrees. Fill out the diagram below and figure out how fair the ball goes, and the maximum height it can achieve.

Bonus: Is it going to fly over a goalpost 10 m away?

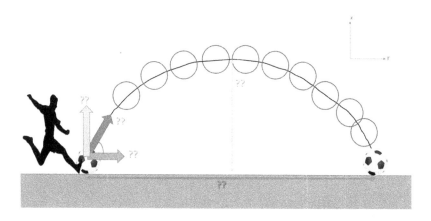

Challenge 3 – Answers

Based on the equation for maximum vertical height, we get:

$$H = \frac{u^2 \, (sin \, \theta)^2}{2g}$$

$$H = \frac{100(sin \, 45)^2}{2 * 9.8} = 2.55 \, m \, high$$

Based on the equation for horizontal range, we get:

$$R = \frac{u^2 \, sin \, 2\theta}{g}$$

$$R = \frac{10^2 \, sin \, 90}{9.8} = 10.2 \, m$$

So, the ball travels a maximum height of 2.55 m before coming down. And it achieves a range of only 10.2 m.

So, it does not go over a goalpost 10 m away. The goalpost's height is 2.7 m but the maximum height the ball achieves in only 2.55 m.

Challenge 4

The ball is moving at a speed of 20 mph. The wind is blowing against the ball at a speed of 6 mph. What's the absolute and relative velocity of the ball?

$V_{ball,rel}$ = ??
$V_{ball,abs}$ = ??

V_{ball} = Ball Speed = ??

Challenge 4 – Answers

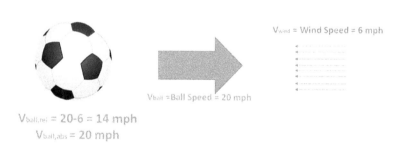

V_{wind} = Wind Speed = 6 mph

V_{ball} = Ball Speed = 20 mph

$V_{ball,rel}$ = 20-6 = 14 mph
$V_{ball,abs}$ = 20 mph

Challenge 5

A ball is moving at a velocity of 37 mph in the direction of wind. The wind is blowing at 10 mph. What is the absolute velocity and relative velocity of the ball?

V_{wind} = Wind Speed = ??

V_{ball} =Ball Speed = ??

Draw Wind above

$V_{ball,rel}$ = ??
$V_{ball,abs}$ = ??

Challenge 5 – Answers

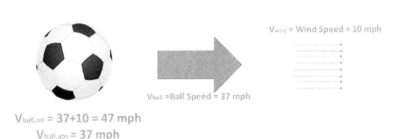

V_{wind} = Wind Speed = 10 mph

V_{ball} =Ball Speed = 37 mph

$V_{ball,rel}$ = 37+10 = 47 mph
$V_{ball,abs}$ = 37 mph

Challenge 6

Here's the ball with the wind flowing against it. In the empty sheet below, draw the areas of high and low pressure and the direction it is likely to bend.

Challenge 6 – Answers

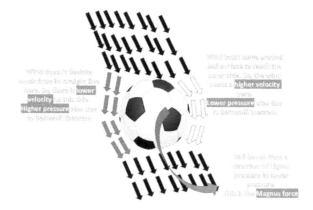

Challenge 7:

Challenge 7 – Answers

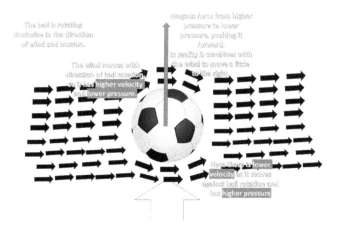

Challenge 8:

In the example above, the ball hits both hands at 50 m/s and both keepers punch the ball back at 10 m/s (the ball is 10 m/s after the punch). The ball contacts Goalkeeper A's hands for 0.05 seconds while it is in contact with Goalkeeper B's gloves for 0.5 seconds. What is the force applied on Goalkeeper A's hands and Goalkeeper B's gloves? Complete the free body diagram below and calculate.

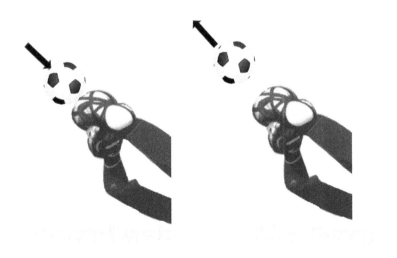

Challenge 8 – Answers:

So, we have:

m = 0.41 kg

u = 50 m/s

v = -10 m/s (it goes in opposite direction so -ve sign)

$$F = \frac{m(v - u)}{t}$$

$$F_A = \frac{0.41(-10 - 50)}{0.05} = 492 \, N$$

$$F_B = \frac{0.41(-10 - 50)}{0.05} = 49.2 \, N$$

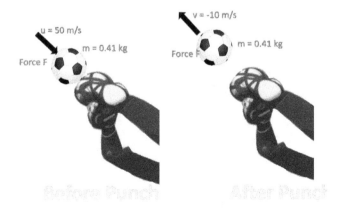

Challenge 9:

Spot Number 2 has the highest chance of a goal.

Challenge 10:

What is the angle that a spot makes between the goalposts. The spot is 15 m away horizontally and 15 m away vertically as shown below.

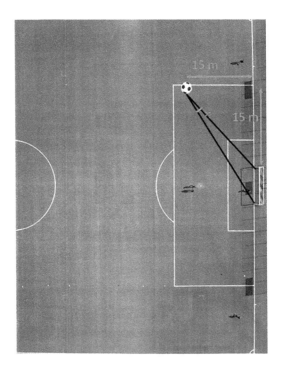

Challenge 10 - Answers:

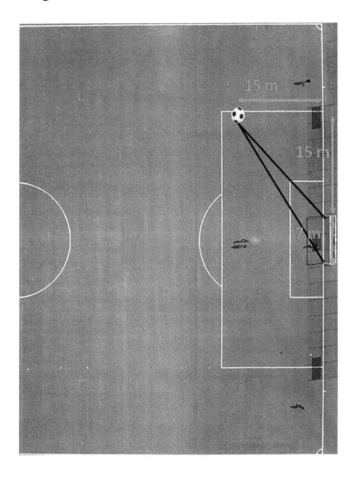

$$\tan^{-1}\frac{22}{15} - \tan^{-1}\frac{15}{15} = 10.71°$$

Challenge 11:

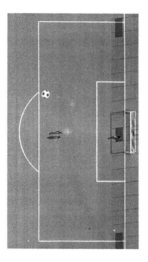

Challenge 11 - Answers

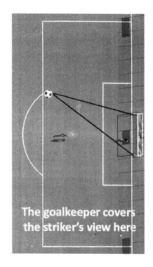

The goalkeeper covers the striker's view here

Challenge 12:

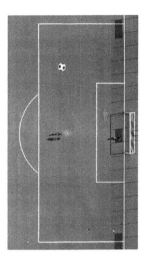

Challenge 12 - Answers

Challenge 13:

Challenge 13 - Answers:

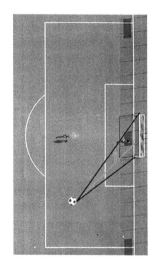

www.ingramcontent.com/pod-product-compliance
Lightning Source LLC
Chambersburg PA
CBHW070845070326
40690CB00009B/1705